THE
ALPHABETICAL
CITY

PAMPHLET   ARCHITECTURE #5

NEW YORK / SAN FRANCISCO

ISBN 0-910413-16-9

Library of Congress catalog card number: 80-80957

THE

ALPHABETICAL

CITY   )

"A word outside of the mind
is a set of dead letters."
From "Language to be looked at,"
Robert Smithson, 1972·

In the alphabetical city— the contiguous portions of cities that evolved on gridiron plans—certain letter-like buildings recurred. The "U", "E", "L", or the "T" type depend on their adjoining structures for meaning. They become "dead letters" when left stranded as free-standing buildings.

This pamphlet searches for the conceptual cement binding urban planning and architecture. It is in two sections. The first concerns different building types which evolved on and defined grid patterns in cities. The second catalogues a variety of grid types.

This research focuses on the mass of construction which completes the geometry of the streets and open spaces of modern cities. It is a catalogue limited to unmonumental urban buildings (in the United States) of roughly the first half of the twentieth century. Any generalization of such broad scope will recall H.G. Wells's predicament when he was asked to give a "general outlook" on his travels in America: he "felt like an ant crawling over the carcass of an elephant."

The purpose of this pamphlet is twofold. It stands as a catalogue in the search for buildings suited to gridded cities. It also inquires into the vexing theories and practices of modern planning. This examination does not require that existing building types be replicated literally. To the contrary, the return to previous techniques would be opposite to the manner in which these types initially emerged. It is important to decipher the elements — the ABC's — of making architecture within modern cities. The intention is to collect existing built works without an a priori theory, then study them to probe for a thesis-antithesis of building in the gridded city.

Today, plans to reform modern architecture deal with the development of alternative styles, facade treatments, or ornamental possibilities employing discarded historical references. As a contribution to ongoing debates, this collection concentrates on the relationships of building plans to sections and how they affect and define the underlying physical pattern of cities. Historic building patterns and their evolution into modern building types fostered by development of the elevator and steel frame construction is evidence against the necessity of urban fragmentation realized in the cause of modernity.

A catalogue of buildings that supported varieties of grid patterns is in turn an examination of the grids themselves. This research was done with the belief that the original grid patterns of American cities were idealistic; that they lay a foundation that provided maximum freedom for each individual part. Today, as ideals are subverted toward manipulative ends, this pattern of growth left unattended reflects an atrophy.

This catalogue is offered respectfully to mayors, planning department officials, developers, investment bankers, zoning law makers, and students of architecture as a reassessment of historical urban building patterns.

Steven Holl, February 29, 1980

CONTENTS

As individual buildings in a city are sustained and completed by the lines of surrounding buildings, the fabric of a city takes form. City fabric is defined as urban solids and voids arranged to form continuous patterns of blocks and spaces as opposed to individual buildings placed over the landscape. The urban solids of the fabric develop in accordance with voids of circulation and open space. They are conditioned by the limits of street and lot lines together with the internal limits of building sections.

In 1927 Ludwig Hilberseimer wrote, "the architecture of the large city depends essentially on the solution of two factors: the elementary cell and the urban organism as a whole." Hilberseimer's twofold observation, like the alliance between grids and buildings studied here, is dependent on a third factor introduced during the twentieth century — the strain that technical advances brought to traditional urban patterns.

Acting interdependently, the development of the elevator, steel frame construction, and electricity transformed the common building types of cities. Prior to the twentieth century the growth of the common solids of the city was primarily horizontal. In the twentieth century these solids stand up, altering the continuous profile along the horizon. The impact of this development was most visible in contrast to the medieval tissue of old world cities. On grid patterns in new world cities, this technological factor was often an improvement, adding a vertical dimension to the regularity of the gridiron plan.

From the 1880s through the 1940s there evolved a contiguous architecture unique to gridiron cities across North America. Determined by the pre-existing gridded town plans, individual buildings were extruded from their rectangular plots. With few exceptions, they rose directly from the building line, thus defining the wall of the street. A contiguous fabric was formed as these buildings rose next to one another from adjacent plots. They evolved with three distinct surfaces. Some defined the street edge, some adjoined adjacent buildings, and some defined interior courts.

In these three fundamentally different walls the elements of an urban fabric can be observed. Adjacent walls depend on adjacent construction, thus making street facades the walls of the public space. Interior court facades are the walls of the private court space. These buildings do not have independent continuity of form; instead, each facade responds to differing adjacent conditions in the city. Only when building plots for one edifice comprise an entire block can independent continuity of form in exterior facades be achieved while the city pattern is adhered to.

During the 1940s and 1950s, the evolution of contiguous building types in gridded cities was displaced. Why the change took place is a question involving complex forces whose analysis is beyond the subject of this pamphlet. However, many of the factors which initially set forces in motion, altering building patterns and ultimately fragmenting cities,

have now changed or disappeared. Today we have the dilemma that while the factors have changed, anachronistic reasoning remains in the form of city zoning laws, shaping current development. An example will demonstrate the effects of one small factor and the problematic consequences of its disappearance.

In reaction to tuberculosis epidemics in the early 1920s, sanatorium building programs were begun. With similar logic, planners formulated new programs for apartments that stood free from one another in park settings, maximizing exposure to sunlight and fresh air. The urgency of new programs was aggravated by the necessity to reconstruct a war-devastated Europe. However, other forces were in motion to remedy the cause of the tuberculosis problem.

In 1943 Penicillin was put to use and in 1945 Waksman discovered streptomycin; tuberculosis could be countered directly with drugs. Sanatorium programs were phased out, yet their logic was retained within the housing programs. What was formerly a progressive step became untenable.

A Sanatorium. Patients receive treatment of oxygen supplied at higher pressure than normal.

Cleveland, Ohio, c. 1930

Many factors which originally provoked the break from grid patterns a few decades ago have now changed. Attitudes concerning accommodation of increased automobile transportation, viewpoints encouraging extensive air-conditioning systems, and the vision of the free-standing prism-of-glass tower as ideal, have undergone metamorphoses in recent years, giving way to nearly antipodal thinking.

However, the earlier reasoning remains embedded in city zoning laws. Required setbacks from street lines, side setbacks, bulk regulations encouraging perimeter plazas and regulations directing separation of use are some of these problem areas in zoning laws presently in effect. Today the directives which provoke urban fragmentation must be seriously reconsidered. For many cities, these zoning laws should be rewritten.

The Light and Air Dimension.

The light and air dimension, together with the regulating factor of the city grid pattern, underlie the development of the recurring plan types catalogued here. The need to include natural light and air in buildings became more pronounced as buildings developed to greater heights. Accordingly, apartment, hotel, and office building plans developed on a plan depth of approximately 24 to 50 feet.

In office buildings, heating, air conditioning, and lighting systems supplanted natural light and air requirements. Thus, building plan depths were no longer limited by natural forces and could increase to any dimension.

The Milam Building in San Antonio, designed by George Willis and completed in 1928, has been designated by historians as the first fully air conditioned office block. Yet this structure was designed and built on the commonly used "U" type plan. Evolving mechanical systems hadn't yet influenced the basic building section. In the decades to follow, the development of these systems coincided with the availability of economical energy sources to operate them. Under economic pressures to develop large areas of work space, office buildings were planned with depths of over one hundred feet, as seen in the Number Two Park Ave Building in New York (Buchman & Kahn, Architects, 1929). Plans and section thicknesses became so large as to be unworkable without the systems. They have dark zones of internal space that are mechanically lit and ventilated. The term "hermetically sealed" described these structures without openable windows. At its most extreme, a hermetically sealed building can be a totally windowless office tower.

Today increasing costs make it uneconomical to operate buildings which consume large amounts of power. Structures built before extensive dependency on mechanical systems can now be examined for fundamental solutions to the problems of lighting and natural ventilation. Merely copying old models, however, may prove impractical as cost/efficiency comparisons must be made between the increased exterior surface of a shallow-sectioned light and air building compared to increased costs in mechanical ventilation. Unfortunately, the psychological factors favoring a light and air dimension may not be apparent in this pure statistical analysis.

The artificially lit zone in many large buildings is often surrounded by a sunlit area with outdoor views. It contains machines for recording, copying, and transmitting information, and the operators of those machines. The building layout can create unproductive attitudes in workers who must spend eight hours per day in these dark inner zones.

In a paper written in 1890, the architect John Welborn Root related the light and air dimension to productivity when he stated, "Experience has demonstrated that all spaces within the enclosure of four walls which are not well lighted by sunshine or at least direct daylight, are in office buildings non-productive." Root goes on to analyze the optimum building depth. "This has been found in Chicago to be not more than 24 feet, assuming the height of the story to be about eleven, the window to be placed close to the ceiling, and the average street width being assumed." The building depth Root describes, when doubled to reflect incoming light from opposite sides, is 48 feet. Because of the comparable street widths due to grid pattern similarities in many cities, this dimension recurred constantly, revealing itself clearly as building heights increased.

This parameter was discussed in Raymond Hood's 1932 article in Architectural Forum concerning the central tower at Rockefeller Center. "Grouped around the center are the elevators and service facilities, and surrounding them on each floor we have sketched the 27 feet of lighted space that experience has proven is the maximum to provide light and air to all parts of the building." The Rockefeller Center building is strict in conforming to this dimension. Its stepped form reflects this principle; as the number of elevator banks diminishes with height, the bulk of the building also decreases. Thus, the 27 foot dimension is adhered to.

Hybrid Buildings

Building type catalogues are normally ordered according to types of uses. However, in this catalogue each category contains examples with differing uses. Building functions in the following examples are oftentimes mixed or changing; the structures collected here are "hybrid buildings" with respect to use. Although there are examples throughout history (the house over the shop is prevalent in many ages and cultures) hybrid buildings developed most rapidly in the twentieth century. In the modern city, building function has evolved from the homogenous to the heterogeneous. Growing densities and evolving building techniques have mixed and piled one function atop another, defying critics who contend that a building should look like "what it is." In the hybrid, form may remain absolute while function is changing and in conflict.

An important factor in modern urban buildings is the ability to accommodate changes in use. In New York City, there are many buildings that have changed in use yet remain comparable in plan and section type. For example, the "H" type structure at 50 West 77th Street by McKim, Mead & White functioned as a hotel for decades. Today its plans have been completely changed within its "H" shell to accommodate apartments.

The "U" type structure occupying the corner at 105 Hudson Street in Manhattan is another example of change in use. Its base has changed from a bank, to a store, to a restaurant. The upper floors served for many years as office space and have been transformed into large cooperative apartments. With respect to use, the structures catalogued in this pamphlet are hybrid buildings.

BUILDING TYPES

The collection of buildings catalogued here is ordered according to a three-staged evolution: early contiguous walk-up types, plan extrusions (or letter-like types) and tower types. In the first stage, the lot size is the predominant factor. In the second stage, the shape of the plan is determinant. In the third grouping, increased height has made sections dominant over plans in characterizing the building type.

Three walk-up types are grouped together here. The Dumbell, the Hourglass, and the Father/Son/Holy Ghost (or Bandbox type) are some of the antecedents of extruded plan buildings. The 25' x 100' lot size in New York City, and the 20' x 13' rear lots in Philadelphia were the foundation for these types.

Technological innovations such as the elevator allowed increases in height. Concurrently, the original lot divisions were combined, creating larger, denser developments. According to plan disposition and limitations of light and air exposure, recurring types began to form. These buildings sit on bases that respond to public needs at the street edge and rise up through several stories that are repetitions of the typical plan.

These letter-like extrusions increased in height to such an extent that sections and elevations predominated over plans. The need for light penetration inside buildings as well as outside, to the public space, limited the height of extrusion-type buildings. Future availability of light to the street level was an objective of the 1916 New York Zoning Law. Extruded buildings adjacent to the street front underlie the twin tower block and stepped tower. Even in the largest buildings catalogued here, contiguous definition of street space is maintained. They exemplify urban development in the first fifty years of modern architecture.

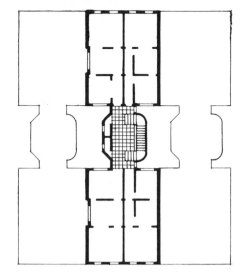

Dumbell Type Tenement, New York
Above example: 1879 competition winner
James E. Ware, Architect

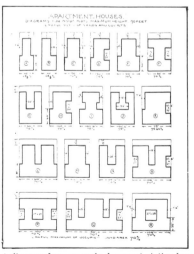

A diagram from an early document stating laws for lot coverage. Every building defines the street. An alphabet begins to form.

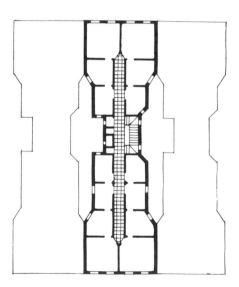

Hour Glass Type, New York, c. 1880
Lot: 25' x 100'

Note: All plan scales are in increments of 10 feet.

7

Waverly Place, Philadelphia

Philadelphia, Pennsylvania

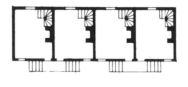

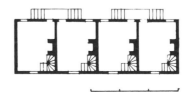

Father/Son/Holy Ghost type, Philadelphia c. 1750.
One room per floor, three floors high, typically
20'x13'. One door, two windows, one stair in
corner. Examples on Manning Street have five levels:
1) sub-basement, 2) kitchen half-level below street,
3) living room, 4) bedroom and bathroom, 5) bedroom

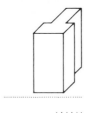

"T"TYPE

As contiguous building types evolved from
dumbells to "T"s, there was a transition from
building on century-old lots (typically 25' x 100' feet
in New York) towards larger ones. Many of the
early "T"s in New York are on plots two lots wide
(50' x 100'). In other cases, two "T"s were built
on three lots, each "T" being 37 1/2 feet wide.
Adjacent lots were often built simultaneously, the
width of the "T" being set by forces other than lot
size, as in the example below.

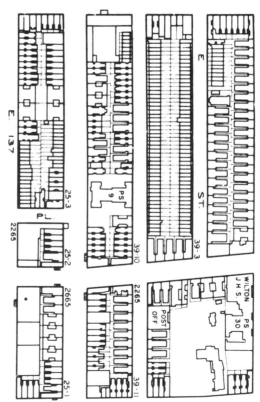

A pattern of existing buildings in the Bronx
Shows types from dumbells to "T"s

9

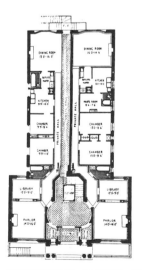

The Rochambeau, New York, 1902
G. A. Schellenger, Architect

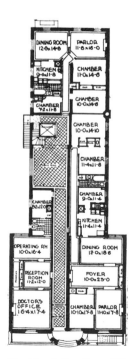

The Allenel, New York, 1908
William L. Rouse, Architect

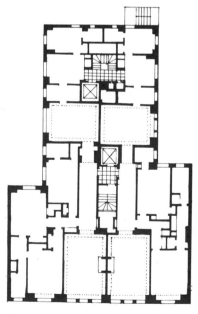

222 East Chestnut, Chicago
Rissman & Hirschfeld, Architects

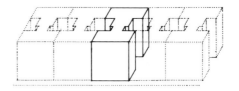

"I" TYPE

"I" TYPE

The "I" type is generally larger than the "T".
In New York City, three contiguous lots often provide
the 75' x 100' plot of an "I". Early structures are
equipped with one elevator and have four apartments
per floor. Other versions of the "I" such as 1430 Lake
Shore Drive in Chicago or the Bush Terminal Building
in New York show its development into tower form.

Adler and Sullivan's Schiller Building in Chicago
exhibited a complex mixture of uses within the "I".
On the main level was the Garrick Theater. Above
were several floors of offices, then the German Club's
private concert hall and kitchen, and atop the attic,
a 29' belvedere for observation.

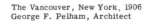

The Vancouver, New York, 1906
George F. Pelham, Architect

The St. Louis, New York, 1905
Lorenz Weiher, Architect

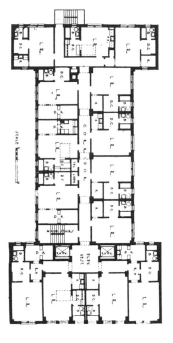

St. James Place Hotel, Chicago, c. 1928
Raymond Gregori, Architect

1430 Lake Shore Drive, Chicago
Robert S. DeGolyer and Company, Architects

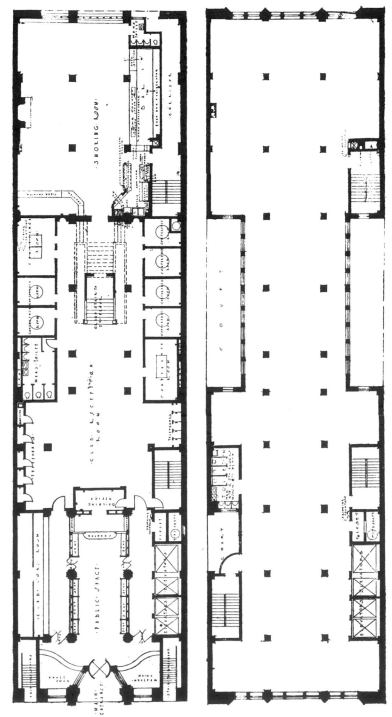

Bush Terminal Building, New York, 1917
Helmle & Corbett, Architects

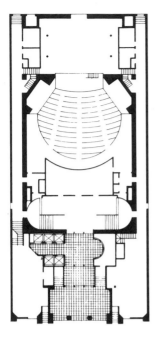

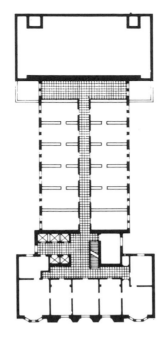

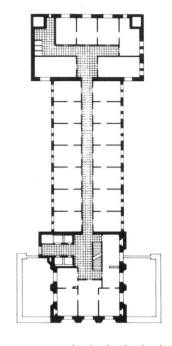

Ground floor

Seventh floor

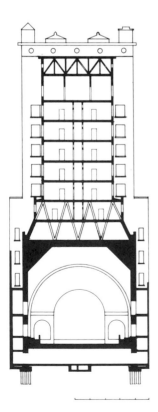

Schiller Building, Chicago, 1892
Adler & Sullivan, Architects

14

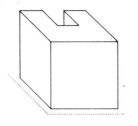

"U" TYPE

The "U" type generally falls into two categories: the open "U", with its court facing the street, and the closed "U", with its court facing the interior of the block. There are instances where two closed "U" types have been built adjoining one another, thereby doubling the dimensions of the interior courtyard. In rare cases, a full courtyard block is created from two closed "U"s. Astor Court in New York is an example. With two architects' statements in concert, both buildings benefit.

One "U" example included here, the Wainwright Building by Louis Sullivan, is important for the discussion that accompanied it. In "The Tall Office Building Artistically Considered," Sullivan wrote, "I am here seeking not for an individual or special solution, but for a true normal type...." Sullivan directed his argument towards the elevation of the type which he said was "a three-part division, not from any theory, symbol or fancied logic."

This argument was advanced during a time when distinct historical building facades were piled upon one another to express a tall office building. He related a base/shaft/top composition to the urban conditions and uses of the building. A ground floor for shops, banks, or commercial establishments fronts the street. Together with its easily accessible mezzanine, it forms the base for "an indefinite number of stories, tier upon tier," crowned by a top space, "purely physiological in its nature—namely, the attic."

Sullivan did not consider the floor plan or light court germane to the problem, although he mentions "in rare instances the plan or floor arrangement... take on aesthetic value, and this usually when the lighting court is external."

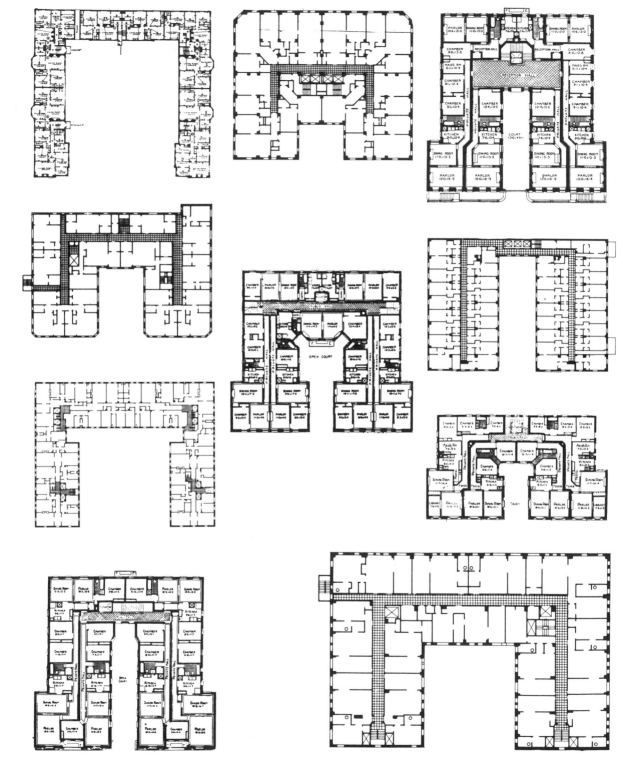

16

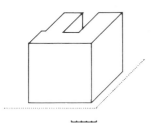

Wainwright Building, St. Louis, 1891
Adler & Sullivan, Architects

From Louis Sullivan.
by Albert Bush-Brown

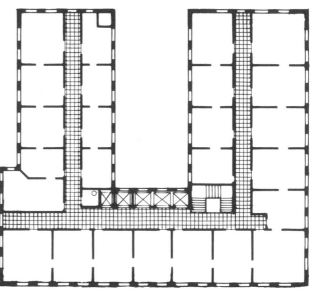

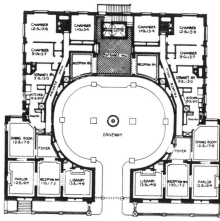

PLAN OF UPPER FLOORS

PLAN OF FIRST FLOOR

Lasanno Court, New York, 1907
Schwartz & Gross, Architects

18

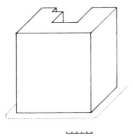 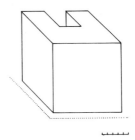

 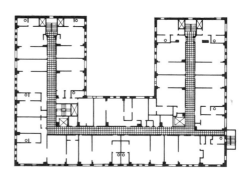

Kenney Apartments, Wichita, Kansas
Schmidt, Boucher & Overend, Architects

Pratt Boulevard Apartments, Chicago
Rissman & Hirschfeld, Architects

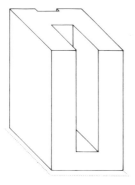

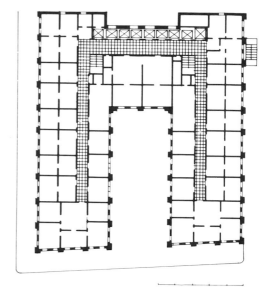

Dime Savings Bank, Detroit, 1918
Graham, Burnham & Co., Architects

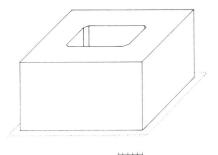

"O" TYPE

Adhering to the lot line at the street edge, courtyard block buildings complete the geometry of the block. The limits of light and air penetration determine their plan depth, typically at 40 to 50 feet. An interior courtyard is thus defined, its breadth and width depending on the underlying block dimensions.

When used for apartments, long internal corridors can be eliminated by making all access ways vertical, using separate lobbies. Security for all lobbies is assured as visitors must pass by the doorman at the courtyard's entrance. Each apartment has two types of view: one to the city outside and another to the garden of the internal court. Some larger rooms (such as those in the Belnord Building in New York) extend the full depth of the plan and are lighted from opposite sides.

The courtyard block type, with street level shops and insular court space, is ancient. Present in many cultures and time periods, the grandest and best known examples are the palazzi of Rome such as the Palazzo Farnese, Palazzo Lancellotti, and Palazzo Sacchetti. The quadrangular plans of the French hotels and the quadrangular courts of Oxford and Cambridge Colleges also exemplify this type.

Modern construction and elevators have permitted increased dimensions. As height increases in a courtyard building, the courtyard should be widened to allow sunlight penetration. However, block size of the city pattern limits this enlargement, making a boundary to its vertical extension.

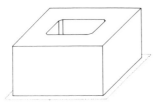
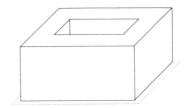

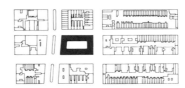

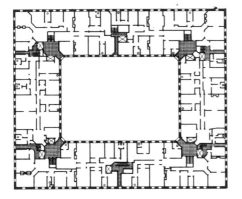
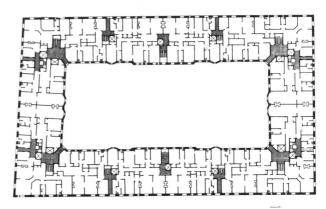

The Apthorp, New York, 1908
Clinton & Russell, Architects

The Belnord, New York, 1908
H. Hobart Weekes, Architect

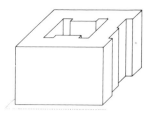
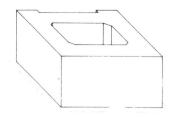

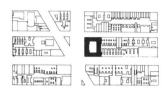

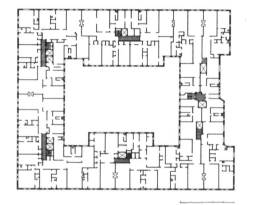
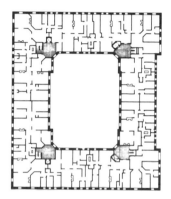

1185 Park Avenue, New York, 1929
Schwartz & Gross, Architects

Graham Court, New York, 1901
Clinton & Russell, Architects

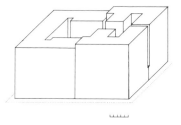

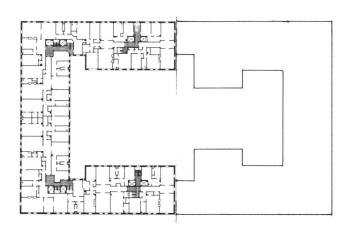

Astor Court, New York, 1916
Charles A. Platt, Architect

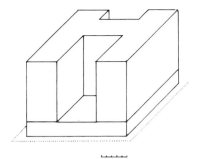

"H" TYPE

"H" type structures often fill an entire city block. While the "I" type concentrates public circulation along the center, in the "H" it is pulled out along the arms. These buildings, like most contiguous types, are shaped by the forces of the street as well as those of the upper floors.

In some cases the upper story plans are antipodal to those at the base. For example the plans of the Equitable Building in New York demonstrates a collision of forces: one set of requirements shapes the cruciform corridors in the ground plan; another shapes the "H" corridors layered repetitively above. In such a case of collision, one can imagine almost any shape of plan sitting atop a base which resolves its street edges with the surrounding fabric.

The Equitable Building is the extreme example of height in the extruded "H"type. It occurred just prior to the New York Zoning Law's sanction of another type— the stepped tower. For typical conditions, extruded buildings reach a limitation at about 20 stories. If a taller structure is required, they give way to more appropriate types. However, the lesson of their resolution of opposites in the base and shaft is still valuable today to anyone building on the city grid.

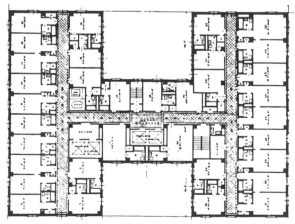

Covington Hotel, Covington, Kentucky
Preston J. Bradshaw, Architect

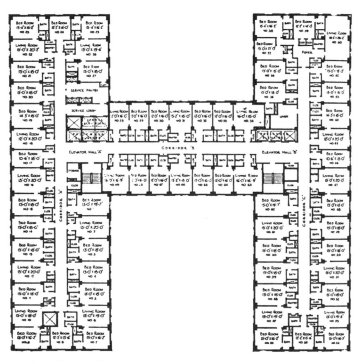

Barclay Hotel, New York
Cross & Cross, Architects

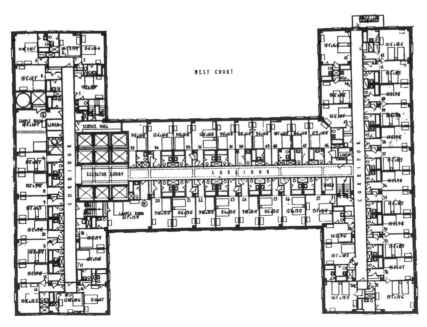

Hotel Schroeder, Milwaukee
Holabird & Root, Architects

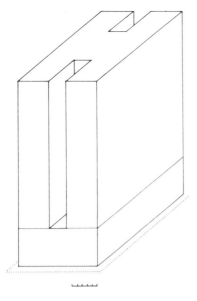

Equitable Building, New York, 1915
E.R. Graham, Architect

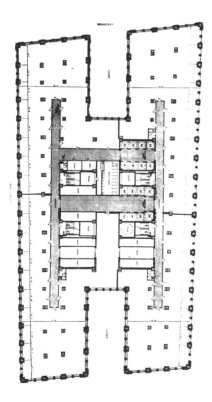

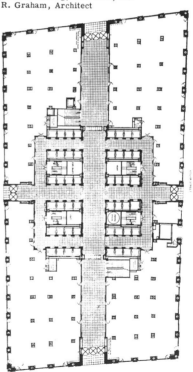

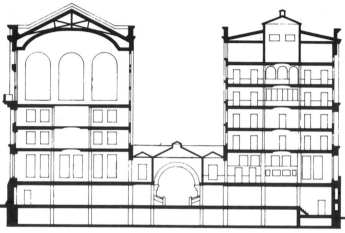

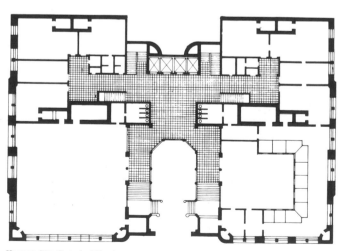

Kansas City Board of Trade
Burnham & Root, Architects

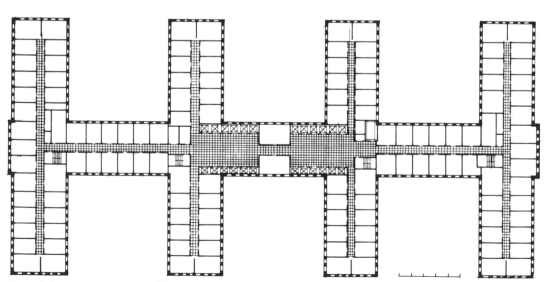

General Motors Building, Detroit, 1921
Albert Kahn, Inc., Architects

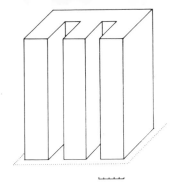

"E" TYPE

The "E" type, like the "U", falls into two categories: one with courts turned away from the street, the other with courts opening to the street. The different orientations are reflected in the contrasting disposition of elements in the plan. In most of the structures catalogued here, elevators and public foyers are located internally, the best naturally lit areas being allocated to rentable space. In the "E" with its courts turned toward the block's interior, the center wing is the most practical location for elevators and foyers (see the Oliver Building, Pittsburgh). In the open "E", with courts facing the street, the rear wall is the likely location (see the Dexter Horton Building, Seattle).

Best advantage of light is taken in an open "E" whose courts face south. In the example of the Dexter Horton Building, the effect of southern exposure is amplified by the white glazed finish of the court walls.

The example of the Russ Building in San Francisco illustrates the transition from the purely extruded types to the tower atop an extrusion. The tower on the "E" shaped Russ Building is comparable to Seattle's Smith Tower atop its "U", New York's Woolworth Building Tower atop its "U", and the Wallick Deshler Hotel Tower atop its "L" in Columbus, Ohio.

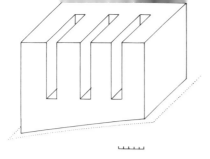

Dexter Horton Building, Seattle, 1922
John Graham, Architect

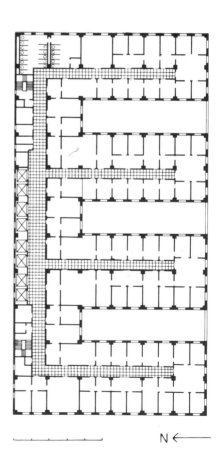

N ←

32

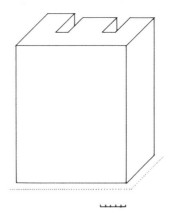

Oliver Building, Pittsburgh, 1908
D.H. Burnham & Co., Architects

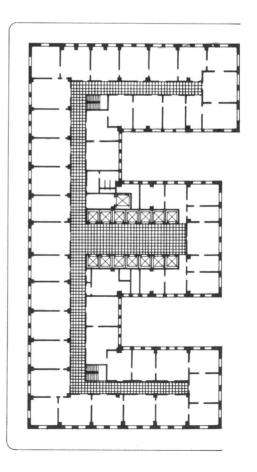

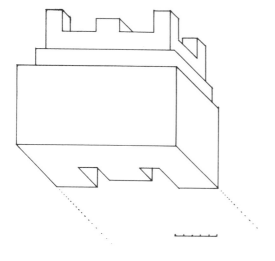

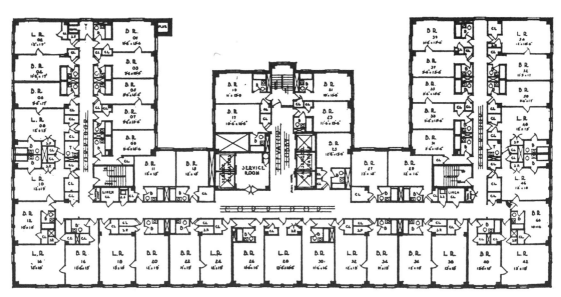

Leverich Towers Hotel, Brooklyn
Starrett & Van Vleck, Architects

34

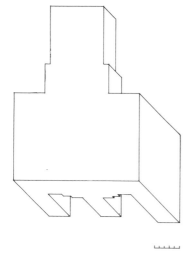

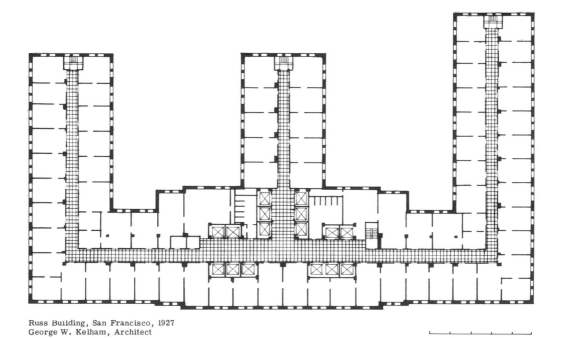

Russ Building, San Francisco, 1927
George W. Kelham, Architect

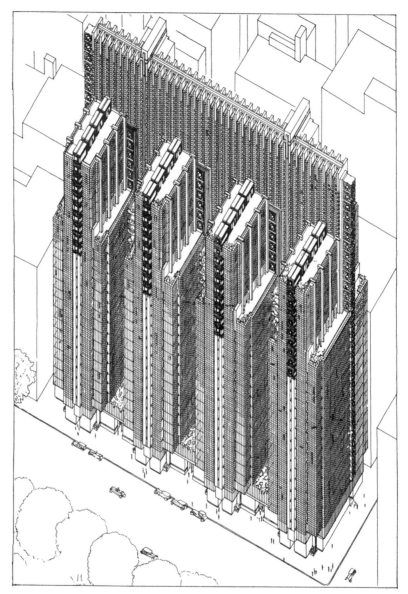

National Life Insurance Co., Chicago, 1920-1925
Frank Lloyd Wright, Architect

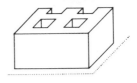

"B" TYPE

The "B" type or binuclear courtyard has definite
limitations. The rooms of a courtyard building large
enough to extend to the perimeter of a city block have
potential views onto the court and the street. The
rooms of the center wing of the "B", however, are
limited to interior views. In the case of the Mills
Building in San Francisco or that of Crescent Court
in New York, the problem of constricted light and
ventilation has discouraged the repetition of this type
on short rectangular blocks.

View into court from lobby

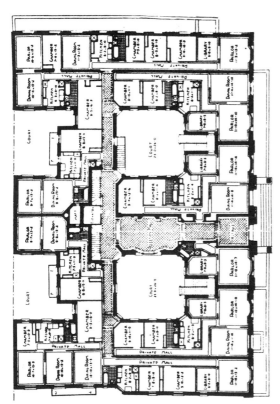

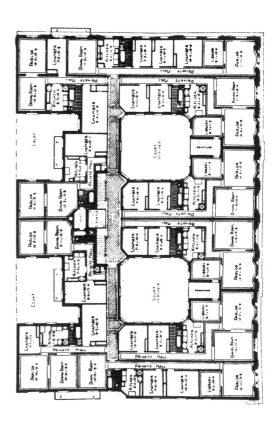

Crescent Court, New York, 1905
Neville & Bagge, Architects

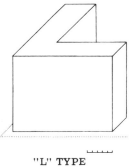

"L" TYPE

The restrictions on courtyard types become more severe as courts become constricted when height increases. The "L", however, can be extended in height without internally set limits. Its successful extension in a contiguous fabric depends on street widths, sun orientation, and adjacent blocks. With two facades defining the wall of the street, the "L" is particularly suitable for the corners of blocks. In the case of the former Wallick-Deshler Hotel in Columbus, Ohio, the condition is further emphasized by the placement of a tower exactly at the corner of the "L".

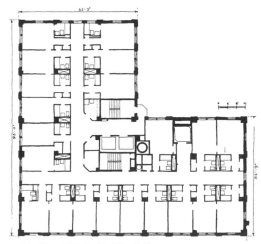

Blue Bonnet Hotel, Fort Worth Texas
Elmer Withers, Mauran, Russel & Crowell, Architects

Asbury Apartments, Los Angeles
Norman W. Alpaugh, Architect

Wallick-Deshler Hotel, Columbus, Ohio
C. Howard Crane, Architect

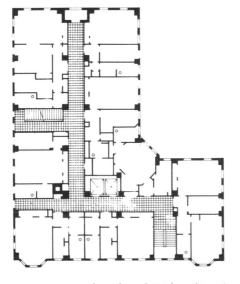

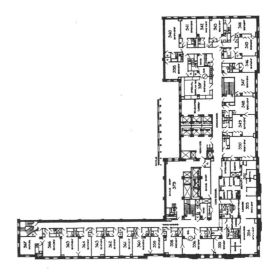

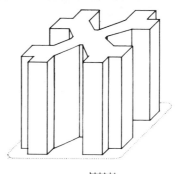

"X" TYPE

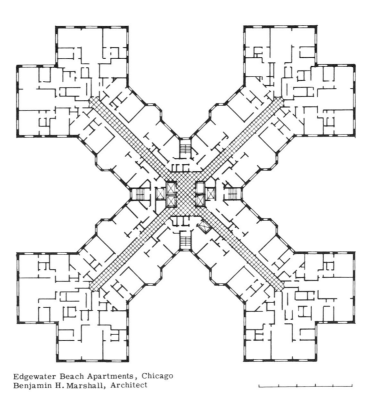

Edgewater Beach Apartments, Chicago
Benjamin H. Marshall, Architect

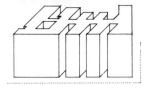

COMBINATIONS

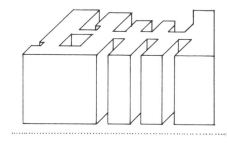

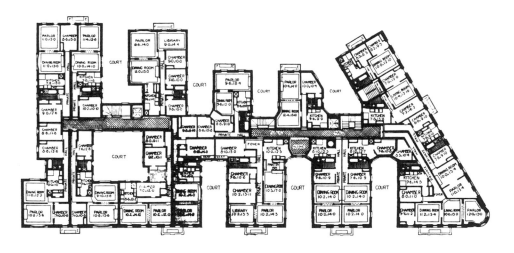

A-RE-CO Court, New York 1906
H. H. Morrison, Architect

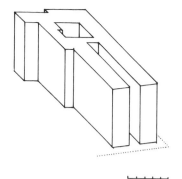

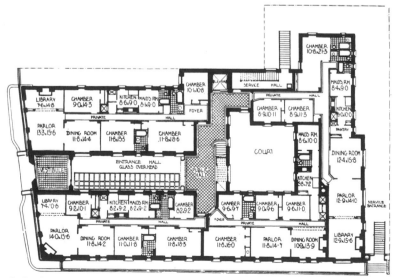

Irving Arms, New York, 1906
H. H. Morrison, Architect

45

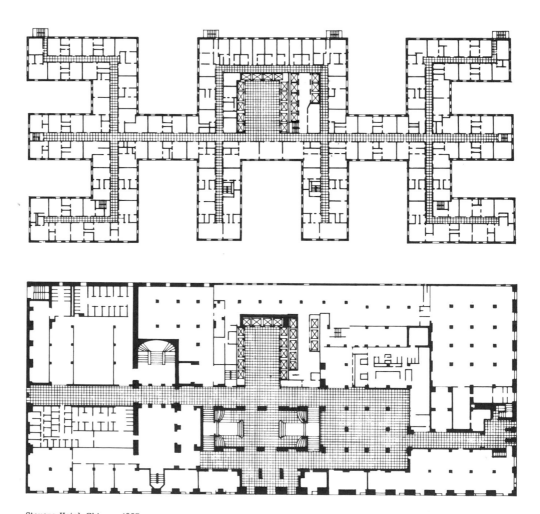

Stevens Hotel, Chicago, 1927
Holabird & Roche, Architects

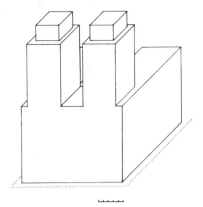

TWIN TOWER BLOCK

Notre-Dame of Paris (from Victor Hugo's novel of 1831): "This will kill that. The book will kill the building." Later in the text: "And in the future should architecture accidentally revive, it will no longer be master. It will be subject to the law of literature which once received the law from it."

In New York during the 1930s, double apartment towers on a base continuous with the street frontage emerged as a modern building type. It developed in response to a coincidence of several factors: 1) options such as a 25% tower allowance under the 1916 zoning law; 2) highly desirable frontage on sites along the western edge of Central Park; and 3) the small dimensional requirements in the plans of towers with two apartments per floor.

The twin tower type evolved rapidly in the modern city, although the image it evoked recalled a memory of many earlier edifices. For example, the ancient Egyptians, with a refined sense of proportion, erected their obelisks in pairs — instead of the single objects often projected by their imitators. The twin towers flanking the entrance to the temple at Baalbek, Lebanon of 2 AD and the towers at St. Riquier en Picardy of 799 AD are early examples. Memory of the great twin towers on the Cathedrals of Notre Dame and Reims, or even the fine proportions of the 13c. towers added to St. Etienne in Caen may be awakened by modern models.

Their thinness plays the mass of one tower against the other; narrow shadows like those of two tall columns rotate with a strip of sunlight between them. Their compositional harmony lies in the geometric proportion of plan to section: the rhythm of one tower played against the other, and the resolution of the towers in the base as it meets and defines the pattern of the streets.

The "experiment" of the rules of the 1916 New York Zoning Law liberated building design. Given a choice between building types, designers could concentrate on the formal and proportional opportunities inherent in the models.

Changes which took effect in the 1963 Zoning Law were caused by factors too complex for review here. However, since 1963 many of these factors have changed. In a search for models of very large apartment blocks which still fit and complement the pattern of the city, these twin tower blocks should not be overlooked.

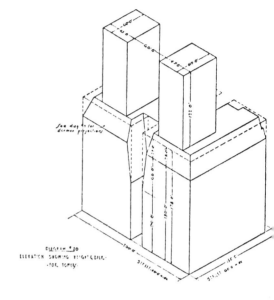

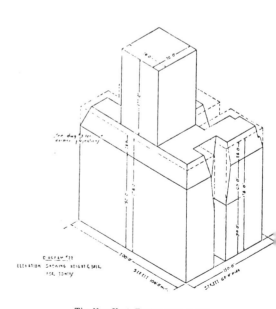

The New York Zoning Law of 1916
A choice with clear limits

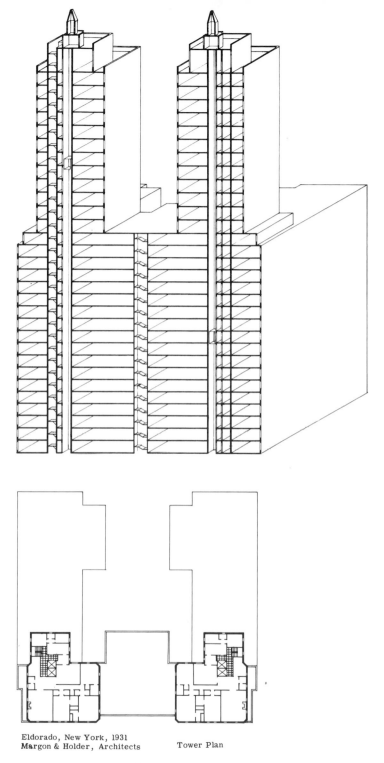

Eldorado, New York, 1931
Margon & Holder, Architects   Tower Plan

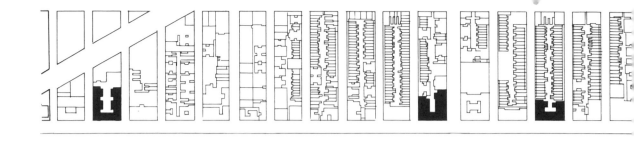

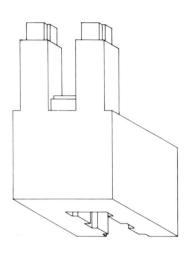

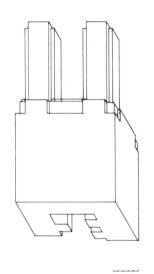

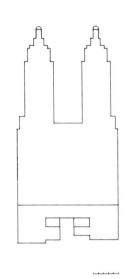

The Century, New York, 1931
Office of Irwin Chanin, Architects

The Majestic, New York, 1930
Office of Irwin Chanin, Architects

The San Remo, New York, 1930
Emery Roth, Architect

50

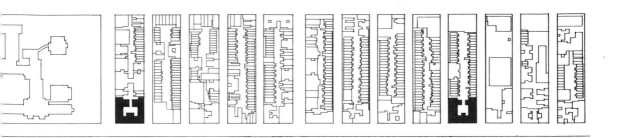

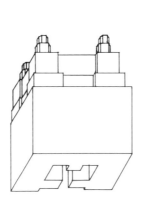

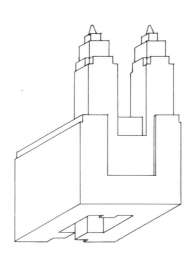

The Beresford, New York, 1929
Emery Roth, Architect

The Eldorado, New York 1931
Margon & Holder, Architects

Indifferent to style, one sees the twin tower blocks aligned on Central Park West as all of one type. Yet looking closer, walking north along the street, we pass the "Ultramoderne" of the Century and the Majestic. Next, the Greek Revival style of the San Remo followed by the Neo-Classical Bereseford which acknowledges formality by adding a tower on 81st Street, becoming twin on two facades. Finally we see the Eldorado which prompted the artist Robert Smithson to note,

> "On top of some of the ultra
> towers we discover ziggurats
> or models of 'cosmic mountains'.
> The heavy leaden memories of
> monolithic civilizations are placed
> out of sight, in the aerial regions
> that few look at...Today's artist
> trys to make his art refer to
> nothing, while the art of the thirties
> seemed to refer to everything.
> But of course, today and yester-
> day may always be reversed."

View into a court.

STEPPED TOWER BLOCK

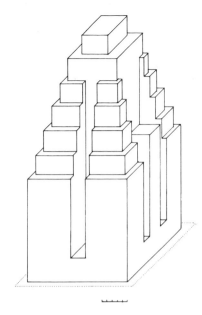

The stepped tower block is a unified, large modern building type stepping down to meet the pattern of the streets and adjacent blocks of the city. The evolution of its section and plan coincides with the technical innovations that gave rise to the skyscraper.

Although the stepped tower block was thrust into modern development under the 1916 New York Zoning Law, its unwritten history is ancient. A "staged tower" was built about 2450 BC as part of the Chaldean Palace, one of Mesopotamia's oldest structures. The Assyrian Palace of Sargon and the platform on which it stands as well as Babylon's "Hanging Gardens" and the Tower of Babel are all ancient precedents. In pre-Columbian America, the stepped and terraced pyramids of Tikal and Teopantepec imprint themselves on the memory as an architectural type whose image is evoked by the modern stepped tower.

In an illustrated 1891 essay, Louis Sullivan introduced the "Setback Skyscraper City" concept while he simultaneously proposed a stepped cruciform skyscraper for Chicago. Here in 1891 is the cruciform skyscraper born in its urban form, stepping up from its base which defines the street walls of the public space. Thirty years later, in 1921, the cruciform model was severed from the street pattern and proposed as a freestanding structure in the Voisin Plan by LeCorbusier. This cruciform of slabs became a symbol of the spirit of "a new city to replace the old," breaking away from the inherited urban patterns in cities across the globe. Today, in a spirit of reform, it is reassuring to see the dynamic urban potential of Sullivan's original cruciform.

In 1963 the New York Zoning Law of 1916 was changed. The stepped tower was discouraged and the freestanding tower, set back from the street, was heralded as the new model. Anti-urban theories germinating in Europe had finally permeated and altered the development of a modern urban fabric in America. Today the fragmentation of original urban patterns in most American cities—the loss of street-aligned shops, undefined side plazas surrounding freestanding towers, and wind turbulence at street level— call for the reconsideration of a modern urban type: the stepped tower block.

Sketch for a castle by Leonardo da Vinci.

New Yorker Hotel, New York, 1930
Sugarman & Berger, Architects

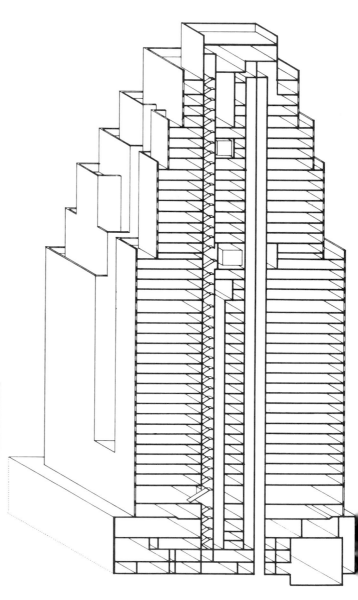

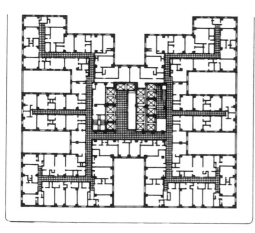

5th to 20th floors

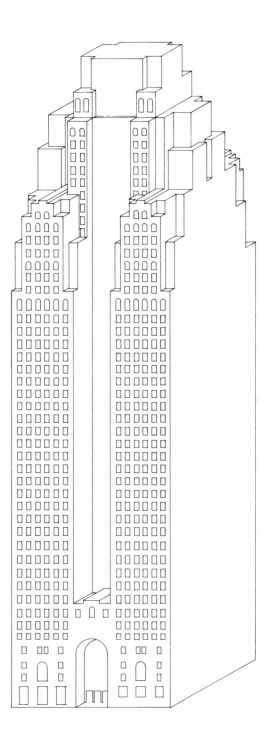

Penobscot Building, Detroit, 1928
Smith, Hynchman & Grylls, Architects

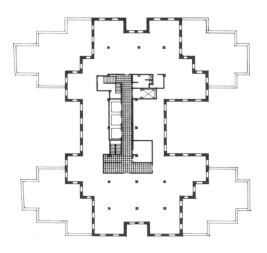

55

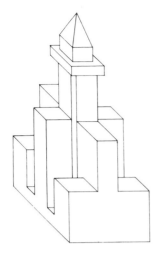

Fraternity Temple, Chicago, 1891 (Project)
Adler & Sullivan, Architects

Larkin Building, New York, proposed 1926
John A. & Edward L. Larkin, Architects

56

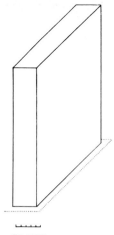

SLABS

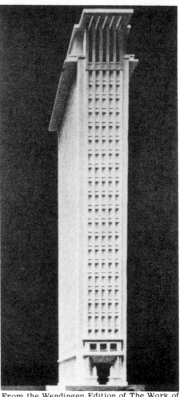

Project for a Skyscraper, c. 1915
Frank Lloyd Wright, Architect

From the Wendingen Edition of The Work of
Frank Lloyd Wright, c. 1965 Olgivanna Lloyd Wright

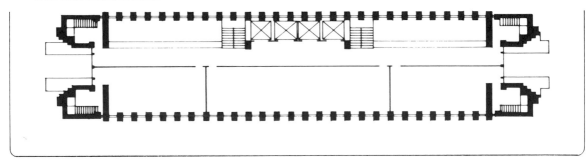

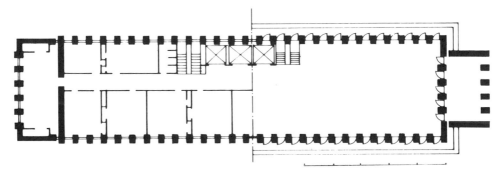

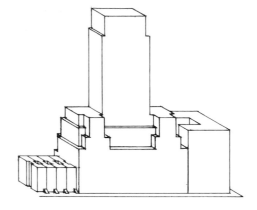

GENERAL OBSERVATIONS

Selected historic structures in the active modern city can be restored without forbidding new construction to the entire "historic area." If the geometry of the original street pattern is adhered to, a new edifice need not break rank with an existing order. New structures can support older edifices by their alignment along the wall of the street. The liberating aspect of the grid is thus expressed; it accommodates many ages and epochs simultaneously.

As shown in the above diagram, all sections of the buildings studied here— the Dumbell walk-up, a "U" type, and a stepped tower— can exist on the same city block.

Economy in the distribution of utilities is realized in urban density as compared to the high cost of long suburban mechanical lines. Adjacent walls in urban fabric structures prevent buildings from dissipating heat to the atmosphere as do their free-standing suburban counterparts. Efficiency of transportation in a live-in city eliminates commuter transportation. Efficiency of a social life is facilitated by the meeting space of the street. Finally, any effort to build for the city reduces the cause of urban sprawl. In this sense, building in the city conserves natural terrain and the natural habitat of wild animals.

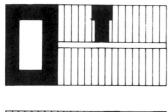
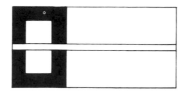

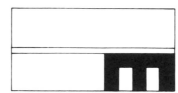

TYPICAL BLOCK SIZES

CHICAGO
300' x 600'
Alleys: 14' and 20' wide

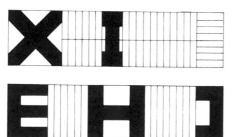
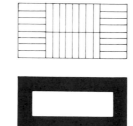

NEW YORK CITY
200' x 800'
No alleys

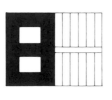

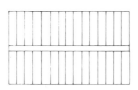

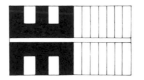

SEATTLE
260' x 360'
Alleys: 16' wide

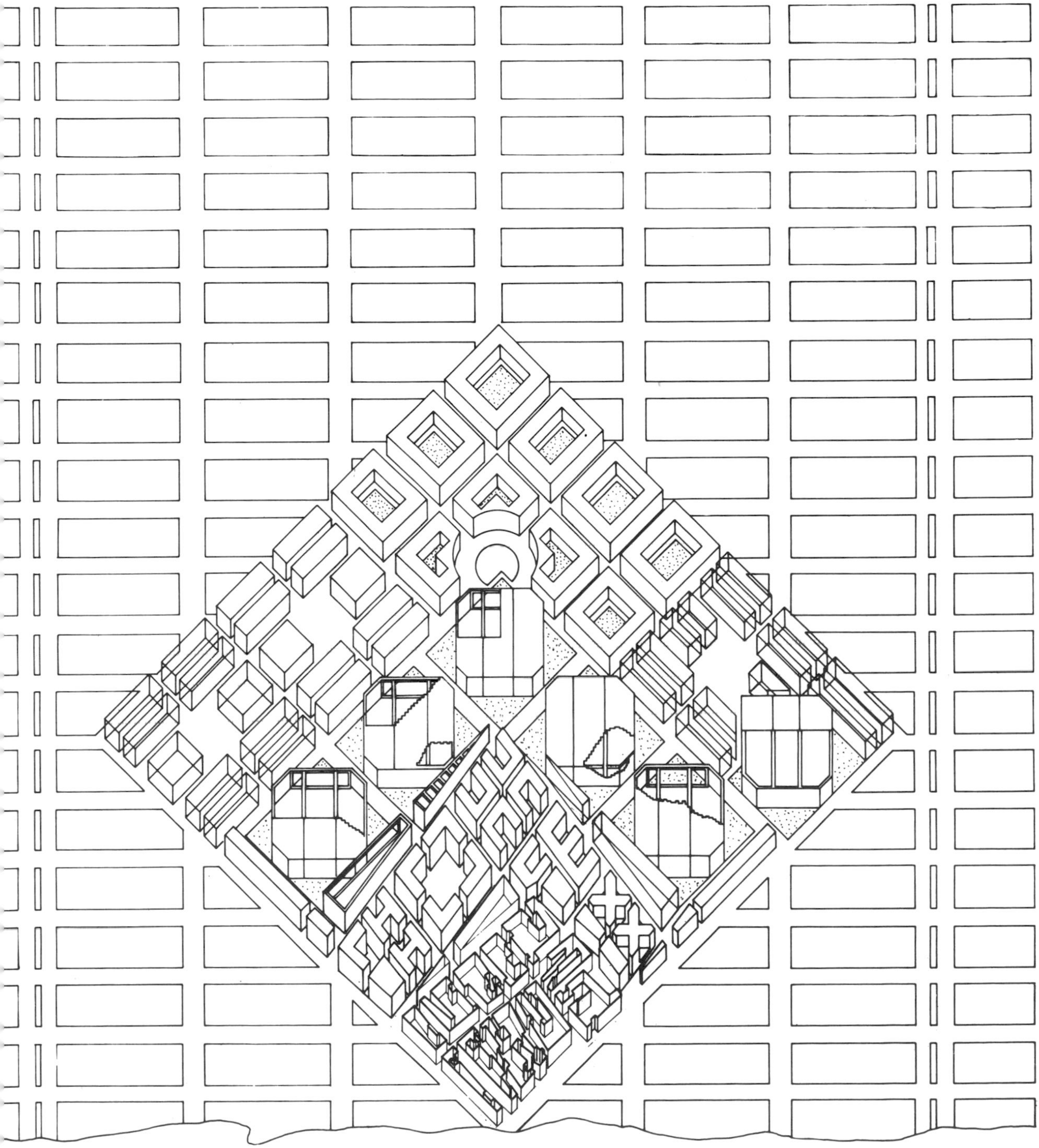

GRIDS COMPARED TO MEANDERS

In the closing decades of the nineteenth century, the prolific and highly esteemed Camillo Sitte argued that geometrical plans should not be imposed on complex historical situations that had resulted in irregular boundary lines. Twenty years later, LeCorbusier argued the reverse, insisting that Sitte had quite simply "posed the problem badly." Another twenty years brought destruction of the ancient historical situations (in many cases by war bombing) and a generation of planners working with the modern attitude of "a new city to replace the old."

In the closing decades of the twentieth century we are seeing an almost literal reintroduction of the forgotten arguments of Sitte. In Europe the relentless work of young theorists in only the past five years has suggested in fact that the modern theorists "posed the problem badly."

Yet this argument and its reverse— the grid versus the meander— has little application in new world cities that were laid out in a single gesture. The earliest cities in America were not complex historical layers of development from path to street; rather, they were immediately grids. They can accommodate the seventeenth or the twentieth century simultaneously. The current reassessment of the ancient precedents of urban space in Europe are inspiring, yet misapplied if brought to the circumstance of the grid plan.

The grid patterns underlying most American cities reflect a single act, not a complex evolution. Although the grids were fixed in a minimum limit, buildings evolving on them reflect an unplanned flexibility. Streets were not designed to lead from one building to another. In these grids, the buildings are shifting incidents of a fixed structural skeleton, like shifting walls in the fixed skeleton of a Japanese house. The buildings are incidents fitted into the space between the streets. Beyond defining the street space at the lot line, the buildings themselves can be seen as manifestations of individual freedom.

In the early American town plans, the grid pattern layouts coincide with the developing view of a worldly order created out of variety. The grids laid a foundation for an order embodying maximum freedom for the individual part. As an ideal, this is a minimum limit, a setting for the unpredictable thesis and antithesis that might come in the expressions of the buildings themselves according to their builders or owners.

New York City

London

One obvious difference is apparent when comparing early American grids to the gridirons of ancient Roman military camps, or the gridirons of ancient Chinese cities. In ancient China the grid had an absolute center from which the emperor could look up and down the main axes. (In ancient Peking the Emperor's throne was elevated, enabling him to remain seated while observing the city.) The Roman camp was a military colony, an autocratic city with the tent of its commander-king at the center. The checkerboard grid pattern of Savannah, Georgia and New Ebenezer, Georgia had multiple centers instead of a single center. Each ward or city section had five blocks around a central square of its own. These cities grew in increments of five block wards, each one with its own center. The underlying patterns of many of the new world cities began to reflect the social revolutions only beginning, as Western culture threw off the rule of aristocracy and began the development of democracy.

The Grid and The Wheel

A gridiron framework of parallel lines is the most efficient way to apportion the space of a compact settlement of rectilinear buildings. The obviousness of the grid is like the obviousness of the wheel. Yet to assume that the grid spontaneously recommends itself to the town builder may be as narrow as to assume that it is an unfortunate or uninteresting device. Where, then, did the grid originate?

D. Stanislawski wrote an article in 1946 entitled "The Origin and Spread of the Grid Pattern Town" in which he opened with remarks that although many geographers had written on the origin of town patterns and functions, no article had yet been devoted to the origin of the grid. Needless to say, Stanislawski is vague, as are articles relating the origin of the wheel to Mesopotamian potters' wheels.

The ancient Mesopotamian potter, sitting at his fresh invention, spinning wet clay, has an accident. The new device spins off the axle and rolls across the floor of the courtyard in a straight line. The wheel is accidentally born in the second half of the Fourth Millenium BC, and with it the straight line of the grid. Who can deny that the meandering path evokes the image of a foot or hoof in the same way that the straight line evokes the wheel?

These observations leave us to ponder the idea of progress. Today we might agree with Professor Morris Ginsberg that "advance in one direction is frequently accompanied by retrogression in another."

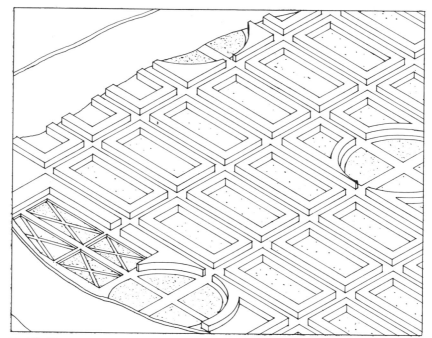

Franklinville, Kentucky, 1796 (projected plan)

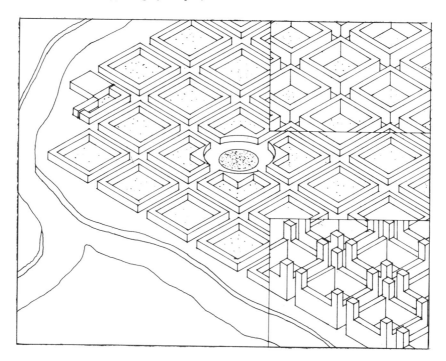

Lystra, Kentucky, 1796 (projected plan)

CHECKERBOARD GRIDS

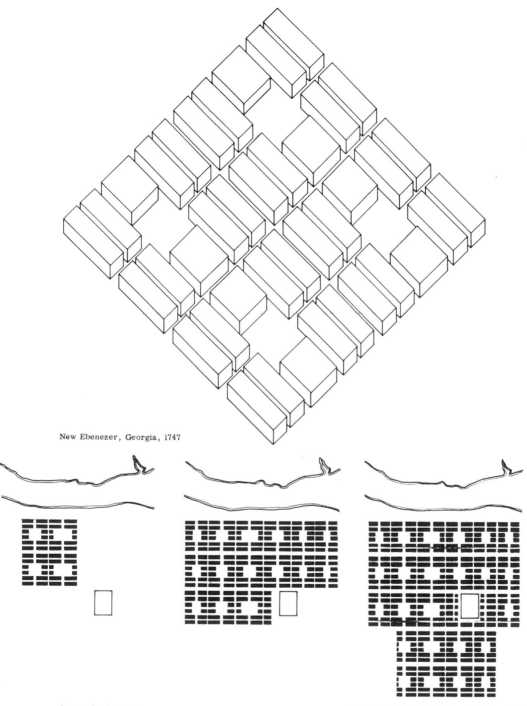

New Ebenezer, Georgia, 1747

Savannah, Georgia
Stages of growth: 1733, 1815, 1856

Information for the grid figures is from Professor
John W. Reps, The Making of Urban America

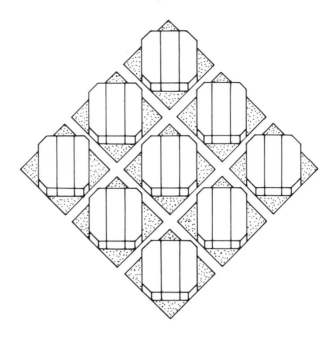

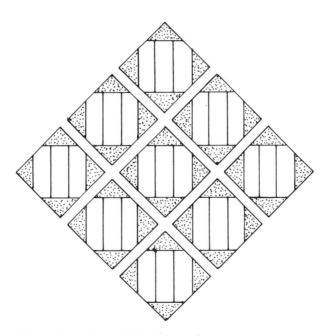

Jeffersonville, Indiana, 1802 (projected plan)

Plan for the Margravate of Azilia, Georgia, 1717 (projected)

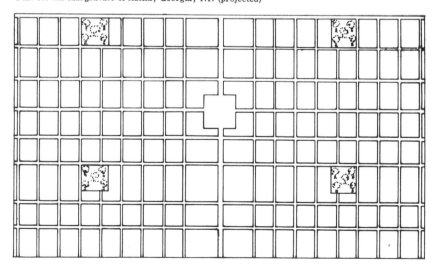

William Penn's Plan for Philadelphia, 1682

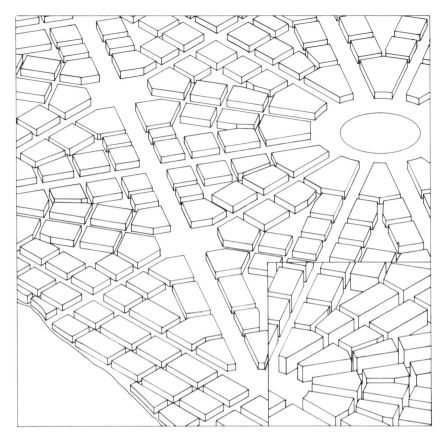

1807 Plan for Detroit, Michigan by Augustus Woodward.
Blocks are elevated to a height of 60' (150' in inset).

This plan is made up of many Sections, each containing six triangular portions radiating from a central Circus. In such a city, growth would be by section, each with its portion of public spaces. Three types of open spaces are envisioned: 1) the Grand Circus, at the intersection of 12 avenues; 2) the rectangular public spaces at the intersection of every 6 avenues; and 3) the central portion of the blocks with their triangular places for public activity to be "planted with trees or otherwise improved and ornamented."

The plan provides a hierarchy of street widths. Avenues would be 200' wide, main streets 120' wide, and minor streets 60' wide. Every lot has rear access. The riverfront edge of the radial grid is straightened to a rectangular grid, providing views onto the water and meeting the needs of port warehouses.

From 1807 to 1824, Woodward's plan was gradually obliterated by General William Hull, newly appointed Governor of Michigan. Woodward's last request on leaving office as Territory Judge was a general plea for town planning as a public art.

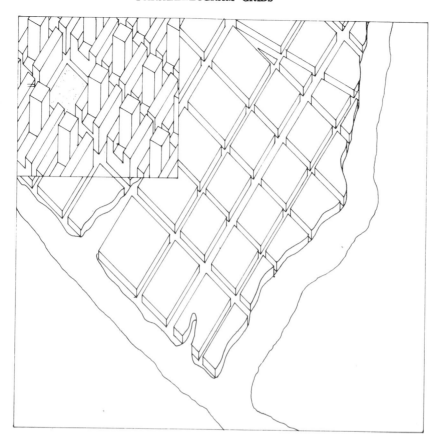

Plan of Marlborough, Virginia, 1691
Projected development with New York Telephone Building.

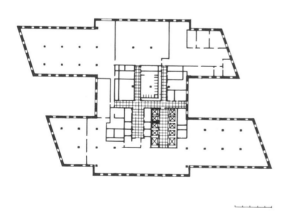

New York Telephone Building, New York, 1926
McKenzie, Voorhees & Gmelin Architects

New York Telephone Building.
Arcade at street level.

CONCLUDING NOTES

The Alphabetical City

In the ABC of Reading, Ezra Pound wrote "that music begins to atrophy when it departs too far from the dance; that poetry begins to atrophy when it gets too far from music." In the twentieth century we have seen architecture begin to atrophy when it gets too far from the city. The Alphabetical City is not a theory nor is it a definitive statement about architecture or urbanism. Rather, it is a collection of examples aimed at understanding one in terms of the other. This is part of an ongoing search for elements, or ABCs of a modern urban architecture. This search, a reconsideration of the architectural element in cities, probes an architecture in which each object is subordinate to a larger whole. An individual building is to the continuous space of a city as a letter is to a sentence or a word. Syntax here does not concern elements within a building, but the syntax of buildings within a city.

To develop a contiguous urban fabric in modern cities will often depend on the rewriting of local zoning laws. Arguments begun earlier this century in Europe advocated constructions standing free of inherited urban patterns. This led to the breakup of an evolving continuity between buildings and city patterns. Inquiry today shows that much of the initial reasoning and many of the causes for these theories have disappeared or changed. With the results of modern planning in front of us, it is obvious that reform is in order. This is urgent if we are to build in concert with the remaining fragments of earlier fabric. Today, in many cities it is unlawful to build in a way that completes the geometry of the streets and public spaces. The logic of anti-urban theories remains embedded in the city planning laws of most towns. Ultimately, the reform of modern planning will be the work of enlightened mayors, planning department officials, and private entrepreneurs.

Building Versus Architecture

What is architecture and what is merely building? Given a set of modern building types or guidelines of the plan and section shapes which fit and complement a city, any construction manager can make a building inducing effects elicited here.

A critical reader will realize that this pamphlet is not about architecture. Problems of light, shade, color, scale, proportion, materials, and the feeling with which they are assembled are not the concern of the construction manager. Yet it appears that an architect adept in orchestrating these effects may still fall short of architecture. Architecture has a concept. It has what Immanuel Kant described as "the unity of rule by which a manifold of contents are held together and connected with one another."

Today we see much building, perhaps more construction than has ever been seen, and almost no architecture. Architecture seems to be confined to drawings and hope. Can this essentially wordless art—that is, this art that lies just beyond the reach of words—negotiate the barriers of its present circumstance? Should this situation result in apathy on the part of architects? This uncertainty was saluted by Louis Sullivan, when in the last decade of his life he was told of the destruction of one of his buildings. "If you live long enough, you'll see all of your buildings destroyed. After all, it is only the IDEA that really counts!"

71

The research for this study, partially documented here, would have been impossible without the help of the New York State Council on the Arts Architectural Fellowships Program, administered by Educational Facilities Laboratories. This pamphlet is an extension of material originally prepared for the lecture "American City Fabrics," for Syracuse School of Architecture, Syracuse, New York December 6, 1978.

Redrawn plans, sections, and axonometrics are by Joseph Fenton. Research and drawing assistants were Suzanne Powadiuk, Arthur Perkins, George Wagner, and Michael Duddy. Layout was by Jennifer Sage and editing of text by Joshua Katz and Elena Brunet. Photography was by Beckett Logan and the author.

PAMPHLET ARCHITECTURE

Pamphlet Architecture was initiated in 1977 as an independent vehicle to criticize, question, and exchange views. Each issue is assembled by an individual author/architect. For more information, pamphlet proposals, or contributions please write to Pamphlet Architecture, c/o Steven Holl Architects, 435 Hudson Street, 4th Floor, New York, New York 10014.

Second edition published by Princeton Architectural Press, Inc.

Pamphlet Architecture is distributed exclusively by Princeton Architectural Press, 37 East 7th Street, New York, New York, 10003. Telephone (212) 995-9620.

PAMPHLETS PUBLISHED

1	Bridges	S. Holl	1978*
2	10 California Houses	M. Mack	1978*
3	Villa Prima Facie	L. Lerup	1979*
4	Stairwells	L. Dimitriu	1979*
5	The Alphabetical City	S. Holl	1980
6	Einstein Tomb	L. Woods	1980*
7	Bridge of Houses	S. Holl	1981*
8	Planetary Architecture	Z. Hadid	1981*
9	Urban and Rural House Types	S. Holl	1983
10	Metafisica Della Architettura	A. Sartoris	1984*
11	Hybrid Buildings	J. Fenton	1985
12	Building;Machines	R. McCarter	1987
13	Edge of a City	S. Holl	1991
14	Mosquitoes	K. Kaplan/T. Krueger	1993
15	War and Architecture	L. Woods	1993
16	Arch. as a Translation of Music	E. Martin	1994
17	Small Buildings	M. Cadwell	1996
18	A+A+...	J. Knoops/F. Rascoe P. Whang/J. Woell	1996

*out of print